# AUSTRALIAN AND NEW ZEALAND FOOD AND DRINK

includes the Pacific Islands

**Christine Osborne**

The Bookwright Press
New York · 1989

# FOOD AND DRINK

African Food and Drink
Australian and New Zealand
 Food and Drink
British Food and Drink
Caribbean Food and Drink
Chinese Food and Drink
French Food and Drink
Greek Food and Drink
Indian Food and Drink
Italian Food and Drink

Japanese Food and Drink
Jewish Food and Drink
Mexican Food and Drink
Middle Eastern Food and Drink
North American Food and Drink
Russian Food and Drink
South East Asian Food and Drink
Spanish Food and Drink
West German Food and Drink

First published in the United States in 1989 by
The Bookwright Press
387 Park Avenue South, New York NY 10016

First published in 1989 by
Wayland (Publishers) Limited
61 Western Road, Hove, East Sussex BN3 1JD, England

**Library of Congress Cataloging-in-Publication Data**

Osborne, Christine
  Australian and New Zealand food and drink / by Christine Osborne.
    p. cm. – (Food and drink)
  Bibliography: p.
  Includes index.
  Summary: Describes the food and beverages of Australia and New
Zealand in relation to their history, geography, and culture. Also
includes recipes and information about regional specialties and
festive foods.
  ISBN 0–531–18293–2
  1. Cookery, Australian – Juvenile literature.   2. Cookery, New
Zealand – Juvenile literature.   3. Beverages – Australia – Juvenile
literature.   4. Beverages – New Zealand – Juvenile literature.
5. Australia – Social life and customs – Juvenile literature.   6. New
Zealand – Social life and customs – Juvenile literature.
(1. Cookery, Australian.   2. Cookery, New Zealand.   3. Australia –
Social life and customs.   4. New Zealand – Social life and customs.)
I. Title.   II. Series.
TX725.A807   1989
394.1'0994–dc20                        89–33046
                                        CIP
                                        AC
Typeset by DP Press, Sevenoaks
Printed in Italy by G. Canale & C.S.p.A., Turin

# Contents

# Australasia and its people

The region known as Australasia consists of those lands lying in the western Pacific between Southeast Asia and the Antarctic: Australia, New Zealand, Papua New Guinea, New Caledonia and their small islands and reefs.

Many different climatic zones are found in such a vast area of contrasting landforms. New Guinea has an equatorial type of climate with a heavy rainfall. The

*Whether their ancestors have come from far away or have been native for thousands of years, today's Australians learn side-by-side.*

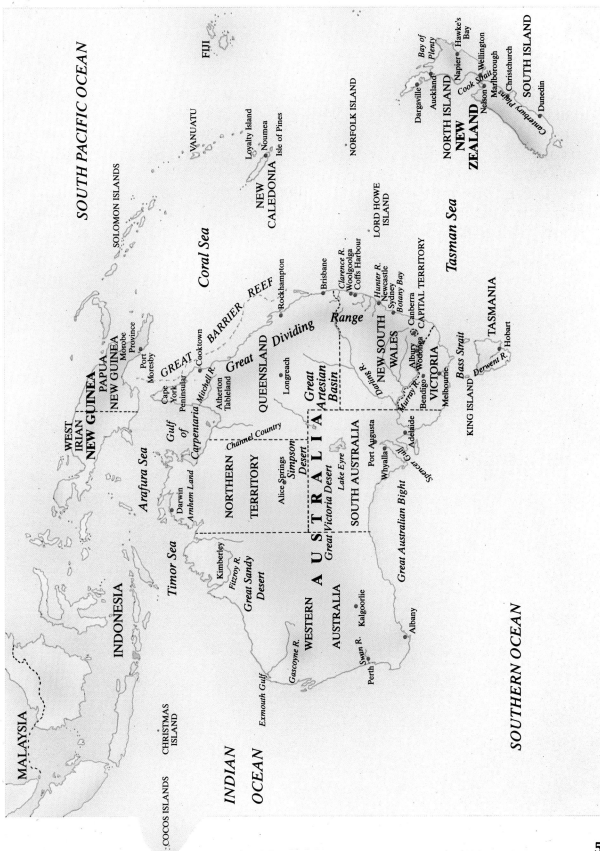

SOUTH PACIFIC OCEAN

FIJI

VANUATU

Loyalty Island
NEW
CALEDONIA
Noumea
Isle of Pines

NORFOLK ISLAND

SOLOMON ISLANDS

Coral Sea

GREAT BARRIER REEF

Brisbane
Clarence R.
Woolgoolga
Coffs Harbour

LORD HOWE
ISLAND

Tasman Sea

Hawke's Bay
Bay of Plenty
Napier
Wellington
Dargaville
Auckland
Cook Strait
Nelson
Marlborough
Christchurch
NORTH ISLAND
NEW
ZEALAND
Canterbury Plains
SOUTH ISLAND
Dunedin

Rockhampton

Hunter R.
Newcastle
Sydney
Botany Bay
Canberra
CAPITAL TERRITORY

TASMANIA

Hobart
Derwent R.

Bass Strait
KING ISLAND

Cooktown
Mitchell R.
Atherton
Tableland

GREAT
Great Dividing Range

QUEENSLAND

Longreach

Great
Artesian
Basin

Darling R.

NEW SOUTH
WALES

Albury
Wodonga
Bendigo
VICTORIA
Melbourne

WEST
IRIAN
NEW GUINEA

PAPUA
NEW GUINEA
Morobe
Province
Port
Moresby

Cape
York
Peninsular
Gulf
of
Carpentaria

A U S T R A L I A

Channel Country

NORTHERN
TERRITORY

Alice Springs
Simpson
Desert

SOUTH AUSTRALIA

Port Augusta

Adelaide
Spencer Gulf
Whyalla

Arafura Sea

Darwin
Arnhem Land

Great Victoria Desert
Lake Eyre

INDONESIA

Timor Sea

Kimberley
Fitzroy R.
Great Sandy
Desert

WESTERN
AUSTRALIA

Kalgoorlie

Great Australian Bight

MALAYSIA

CHRISTMAS
ISLAND

COCOS ISLANDS

INDIAN
OCEAN

Gascoyne R.
Exmouth Gulf

Swan R.
Perth

Albany

SOUTHERN OCEAN

5

*The beach at Byron Bay, the most easterly point in New South Wales. Miles of superb surfing beaches characterize the Australian coastline.*

northern part of Australia, which is almost cut in half by the Tropic of Capricorn, has a similar monsoon season, while the southern portion is more temperate, like most of New Zealand.

Sunshine is the main characteristic of the climate of Australasia, but permanently snow-capped peaks are a feature of New Guinea and New Zealand. There are enormous glaciers on New Zealand's South Island, while geysers and volcanoes occur on the North Island. Like northern Australia, the island of New Caledonia experiences a mild winter with an occasional summer cyclone. The "Top End" (the northern part of the Australian states of Western Australia, Northern Territory and Queensland) usually receives 1 or 2 fierce cyclones a year. The Pacific coast is tempered by southeast trade winds. Violent squalls known as "southerly busters" occur suddenly on a hot afternoon when hundreds of sailing craft are overturned in Sydney Harbor. Occasional bushfires devastate the dry hinterland of the southern states of New South Wales, Victoria and Tasmania, and losses of stock and wildlife are considerable.

Australasia has a unique wild life. The duckbilled platypus, a mammal which lays eggs and suckles its young, for example, is to be found in Australia, while the cus-cus, or sloth, inhabits the New Guinea jungles. Bird life ranges from the dazzling bird of paradise to the flightless emu in Australia, the kiwi in New Zealand and the white cagou, now believed to be extinct, in New Caledonia.

At least two billion years old, Australia is the smallest, flattest continent on earth. Today, Australia has a population of

*Tourists walking the Franz Josef Glacier in the rugged South Island of New Zealand. Mt. Cook, the highest mountain, is permanently snow-capped.*

16,020,000 (including 227,644 Aborigines and Torres Strait Islanders). Its highest peak is Mount Kosciusko, 2,228 m (7,000 ft) high. A narrow coastal plain runs along most of the continent. Where it has not been cleared for settlement and farming, it is a mixture of mallee, or acacia scrub, eucalyptus and rainforest. The Great Dividing Range, 50–150 km (30–90 mi) inland, runs the length of the Pacific coast. To its west, the country is a combination of limestone and grassland, salt-bush and dunes. The great "Deadheart" of central Australia lies on the same latitude as the Sahara Desert.

In the sixteenth and seventeenth centuries, the Portuguese, French, British and Dutch were exploring the uncharted oceans of Australasia. In 1788, a penal settlement was established at Port Jackson, in eastern Australia. The name was later changed to Sydney after the British home secretary, Lord Sydney. Exploration of the interior began in 1813 when the Blue Mountains west of Sydney were crossed by Blaxland, Lawson and Wentworth.

Central Australia took longer to explore. Many courageous men perished in the desert where careless road-travelers risk a similar fate today.

Western Australia lies 4,348 km (2,700 mi) from Sydney, roughly the same distance as between London and New York. A British settlement was founded in 1826 and, like New South Wales, it became a convict settlement. The discovery of gold in Kalgoorlie, in Western Australia and Ballarat-Bendigo, in Victoria, encouraged settlers to go inland.

*The remains of convict settlements on Norfolk Island date from 1825. The island lies 1,700 km (1,060 mi) northeast of Sydney.*

*The Maoris and representatives of Queen Victoria signing the Treaty of Waitangi.*

When the transportation of convicts ceased in 1868, many former prisoners were given land alongside farms worked by free settlers. These early days in Australia were characterized by hardship, loneliness and clashes with the native Aborigines, for whom contact with white people meant death, disease and loss of land rights.

The Commonwealth of Australia came into being in 1901 with the federation of the six colonies, or states. The capital is Canberra in the Australia Capital Territory. Australia administers Norfolk Island 1,700 km (1,000 mi) northeast of Sydney, the Cocos Islands in the Indian Ocean and Christmas Island, a tiny, phosphate-rich island south of Jakarta. A huge area of the Antarctic is administered jointly with New Zealand.

The islands that form New Zealand are outcrops of a continental landmass that sank some 50 million years ago. They are called *Aotearoa*, "Land of the long, white cloud," by the Maoris. The islands are separated by Cook Strait and differ greatly. The South Island has jagged peaks – twenty are over 3,000 m (9,800 ft), while the North Island is thermally active. The Maoris, who migrated to New Zealand from Polynesia around the year AD 900, ceded sovereignty to Queen Victoria in 1840. Today, there are more than 3 million New Zealanders.

During British colonization rough and tough lumbermen and ship builders stripped the lush forests. Whalers, traders and escaped convicts all poured in for their cut of the new colony – mainly land. Conflict with the Maoris over land rights ended in war in 1860. The Treaty of Waitangi still remains the chief source of Maori social and political pressure on the New Zealand government which is based in the capital, Wellington.

In 1774, Captain James Cook named the narrow, cigar-shaped island northeast of Sydney "New Caledonia" after his native Scotland. Other explorers, afflicted with a similar nostalgia for home, called new places by familiar names; for example, New Ireland, Norfolk Island and Stratford on the Avon River.

France claimed New Caledonia in 1853, translating its name to Nouvelle Caledonie. Like Australia, it was used as a dumping ground for convicts. More than 3,000 political prisoners were deported to the beautiful Isle of Pines, lying off the southern tip of the *grand-terre*, or mainland. Following an amnesty in 1879, many returned to France, while others settled locally. Their descendants, known as the Caldoche, grew rich exploiting local nickel mines.

In 1988, New Caledonia's white population, which outnumbers local Melanesians by two to one, voted to remain with France. The struggle for self-determination continues, with disastrous effects on the island's economy. Both New Caledonia and its territories look to Australia for most perishable foods.

Australia has a potentially rich economy based on minerals and agriculture, but economic pressures from overseas greatly influence its balance of payments. Agriculture contributes the largest amount to the gross domestic product, the GDP, or what a country produces. Australia is historically the world's leading exporter of top-grade wool. Today, cross-bred sheep are raised for meat as well as fleece. Meat – lamb, mutton and beef – and wheat are the main exports. The iron and steel industry centers on Newcastle and Port Kembla in New South Wales and Whyalla in South Australia. Other enterprises are shipbuilding, automobile manufacture, textiles, bauxite, petrochemicals,

*Lyttelton, the port for Christchurch, exports produce all over the world.*

aluminum and oil refineries and a range of light industries manufacturing consumer goods.

New Zealand is one of the world's most efficient agricultural producers with 50 percent of its world exports coming from local farms. 74 percent of its electricity needs are supplied by hydroelectric power.

Papua New Guinea was a former Australian protectorate. It has a democratically elected parliament based in its capital, Port Moresby. Administration includes the islands of New Britain, New Ireland, Manus, Buka and Bougainville in the Solomon group.

New Guinea's economy is based on huge copper deposits in Bougainville. Timber, coffee, cocoa, rubber, copra and palm oil are grown commercially, and there is huge potential in local fisheries.

# Indigenous foods

The Aborigines were living on indigenous foods or "bush tucker" for at least 40,000 years before white people came to Australia. Since they did not grow food, an awareness of the environment – its plants and animals – was essential. These hunters and gatherers had a deep understanding of the bush and its changing seasons.

There are some 4,000 varieties of edible native foods and many are extremely nutritious. *Terminalia ferdinandiana*, or the green plum, is one of the world's richest sources of vitamin C.

More than 500 different tribes

*A girl searching for waterlily corms in an Arnhem Land billabong. She digs her feet into the mud beneath the plants to reach the roots. They are cooked over coals or pounded into a flour dough. Corms are high in fiber and carbohydrate with large amounts of protein.*

*The Aboriginal diet today consists of both indigenous foods and those introduced by immigrants.*

once lived all over Australia. They traveled from place to place describing their routes in "songlines." Children were taught the songlines in order to find their way along the bush tracks.

Everything has potential as "bush tucker" but what one Aborigine might kill for food could be sacred to another. This is because all creatures have a place in the "Dreamtime" folklore.

An Aborigine who eats mangrove worm, for example, cannot eat goanna (the monitor lizard), which is the totem of his tribe who live at Tinonee (the place of sharks) on the New South Wales central coast. Yet another Aboriginal tribe may not be able to eat the curious honey ant whose huge, honey-pot abdomen is relished by people in Papunya, central Australia. Papunya means "honey-ant dreaming."

The Aboriginal men also hunt larger animals such as kangaroos, emus and the big dugong (also called sea-cow, or manatee).

Almost all animals were at one stage caught and eaten – snakes, lizards, possums, bandicoots, wombats and wallabies.

Weapons for hunting varied, but common to most tribes were curved wooden boomerangs used for bringing down birds, spears for killing kangaroos, digging sticks for extracting snakes, and a variety of traps and nets. Poisons – mostly discovered by trial and error – were also used to drug emus when they came to drink at water-holes or billabong swamps. Aborigines are great mimics and can copy native calls of a bird or mammal, luring it close enough to club.

Aboriginal women, assisted by children for whom it is part work, part game, spend hours gathering foods – yams, berries, witchetty grubs, goose eggs, long-neck turtles, wild honey and goannas

*Nutritious fruit and vegetables, native to the Pacific Islands, being sold at a local market.*

(said to taste like chicken). Food is carried back to camp in wooden bowls, or *coolamons*, woven fiber bags and baskets made from paperbark. A bamboo, or today a steel knife, is used for cutting, although it is considered just as easy to bite the head off a harmless fat file snake. Toes are used for feeling for pippi shells in the sand, while octopus are plucked from the reef and turned inside out. During foraging trips, women eat berries and shellfish. Mounds, or middens, of oysters and mussels indicated an aboriginal settlement in former times.

The Maoris in New Zealand hunted the native birds – wood pigeon, wood hens and parrots. The giant moa, which was unable to fly, soon became extinct. A common method of capturing birds was by setting up noose snares where the birds came to drink. Early texts mention up to 5,000 pigeons being trapped in a season.

The Maoris, who are skilled at fishing and crafts, also had considerable farming knowledge. As families settled into village communities, they cleared the land for planting rhizomes and the *kumara*, or sweet potato, brought from Polynesia. *Para-tawhiti*, a fern whose large corms were cooked on coals, *taro* or breadfuit, a staple for indigenous peoples throughout Australasia, and *rauriki* or sowthistle, were among other common Maori foods.

# Growing the food

Food production in Australasia has always been a struggle against the elements; heat, unreliable rainfall, leached soil and difficult terrain.

The opening up of Australia to farming is a classic story of pioneers against the bush. Until rivers were charted and ranges crossed, the settlers stayed near the coast where rain is guaranteed. Most Australians still live within the coastal belt, with 84 percent of New Zealanders also living in urban coastal communities.

The growth of inland towns is usually linked to the availability of water, such as at Albury-Wodonga on the Murray-Murrumbidgee river system, or towns in western Queensland supplied from the Great Artesian Basin. Where settlements were originally founded on minerals, like the gold-mining town of Kalgoorlie, water is piped in, often from hundreds of miles away.

Many crops depend on irrigation. Elsewhere, farming is a gamble. Beaten by the drought in Western Australia, a farmer who once ran a 30,000 acre sheep

*An Australian stockman rounding up prime Hereford cattle in New South Wales. On huge plains ranches, motorcycles, or even light aircraft are used for such a task.*

station today sells flowers in Perth for more than he sold sheep. Sheep lose their value very quickly when conditions get tough "Down Under."

Wheat and cattle for meat are the main types of farming in New South Wales. Mixed sheep and wheat farming is common on the southwest slopes. Cereals and rice grow under irrigation in the Riverina. Dairying is confined to the lush coastal plain, especially along the Clarence, Macleay, and lower Hunter rivers. On the New South Wales central coast, Gosford is center of the citrus fruits industry. Farther north, the Hunter River Valley is a rich mixed farming district and center of the oldest wine-producing area in Australia. Coffs Harbor and Woolgoolga on the humid far-north coast grow bananas. Many Sikh migrants own local plantations. Fisheries and oyster-farming are also important.

The tropical state of Queensland supplies a substantial amount of seafood, including the more exotic varieties such as pearl perch, mud crabs and the delicious freshwater barramundi, to southern markets. Trawlers operate from the shrimp centers on the Gulf of Carpentaria in search of the huge tiger and banana shrimp. Queensland is the source of 21 percent of Australia's agricultural produce: tropical fruits, sugar and rice on the coast; dairying, corn and peanuts from the cooler Atherton Tableland.

Cereal crops flourish on the Darling Downs, while beef cattle roam in thousands around the town of Rockhampton and in the Channel Country, west of Charters Towers. In 1987, Australia had an estimated 23.26 million head of prime beef cattle.

Beef is the mainstay of the arid Northern Territory. The introduction of hardy tropical breeds like the Santa Gertrudis has improved local stock. There are some enormous cattle stations with hundreds of thousands of head of stock. Victoria Downs in the Northern Territory is bigger than Belgium. Such huge properties have a unique lifestyle. The family

*Cane barges on the Clarence River, near Yamba on the far north coast of New South Wales. Sugar cane is an important crop in Queensland and northern NSW.*

may only visit the city once a year, and the nearest store may be half a day's drive. There is an increasing demand for water buffalo meat, but hunting them, which is done by helicopter, is rough and costly.

In the huge state of Western Australia, 44 percent is under cultivation with crops and pasture, mainly wheat. The zone around Perth is intensively farmed with potatoes, fruits and vines. The Kimberley Plateau is excellent cattle country, with bananas, sugar and rice grown under irrigation from the Ord river. Western Australia's annual rock lobster catch is worth $90 million a year: Exmouth Gulf is the center of a shrimp industry.

Farming in South Australia is restricted by low rainfall. Sheep and cattle are raised in the north; while rotation of cereals and livestock is practiced along the Spencer Gulf between Port Augusta and the capital, Adelaide. Fruit, vegetables, grapes and pasture are grown along the irrigated Murray River valley. Barossa Valley is one of Australia's best known wine-producing regions. Rich abalone beds lie off the South Australia coast.

The small state of Victoria is Australia's leading producer of mutton and lamb. Wheat, oats and barley are important crops in the Wimmera plains. Mixed farming is carried out in the Murray Valley – cattle and fat lambs on larger properties, and piggeries, poultry,

fruits and vegetables on smaller holdings. Commercial fishing is based on scallops and abalone. Trout, Murray cod and perch are raised in hatcheries.

Salmon farming is an important new enterprise for the island of Tasmania. Atlantic salmon are hatched at Wayatinah in central Tasmania and trucked to the coast where they are kept in ocean cages for 15 months. Some one million fish are produced annually. Tasmania, often known as the "Apple Isle," grows a quarter of

*On the wetlands of Australia's Northern Territory, water buffalo roam wild. Buffalo meat is sold commercially, but slaughtering methods using helicopters are cruel.*

*New Zealand lamb is exported all over the world.*

Australia's apples in the Derwent Valley north of the capital, Hobart. "Stone fruits," such as plums and cherries, are an important crop along with fat lambs, pigs and vegetables.

Lying in Bass Strait between Tasmania and Melbourne is King Island, a small island with a big reputation for high-grade dairy products, especially clotted cream and specialty cheeses.

Like Australia, the story of growing food in New Zealand is one of innovation and adaptation to the climate and terrain. Of several vegetables brought from Polynesia, the Maoris had most success with the sweet potato. Deer, introduced by white settlers, quickly became pests, but venison is now farmed.

While New Zealand has a rich, mixed farming economy, it is best known for sheep, the most successful animal introduced by Europeans, now estimated at some 176 million. Some of the best sheep country in the world is found south of Auckland and on the Canterbury Plains in the South Island. Dairy farming is also practiced, with more than 600 high-grade dairy products marketed abroad. Along with New Zealand lamb, local butter and cheeses are a feature of super-markets throughout Europe and the United States.

The other product found on supermarket shelves is kiwi fruit

*Green-lip mussels are a specialty in New Zealand.*

which is grown mainly around the Bay of Plenty. The hot, dry climate of Hawke's Bay favors horticulture. Across Cook Strait, Nelson is a berry-growing area. New Zealand also produces substantial amounts of honey. One bee-keeping operation covers an area bigger than London.

Seafood accounts for nearly 5 percent of New Zealand trade, mainly orange roughy, or deep-sea perch, salmon, tuna, squid and a variety of shellfish such as green-lip mussels, oysters, and scallops. Trout, which were introduced into the rivers last century, grow to a record size. Trout may not be sold commercially, but hotels and restaurants will cook any you catch.

People living in the Antipodes commonly grow some of their food requirements. Most home gardens feature a plot growing vegetables such as lettuce, tomatoes and beans. In the more tropical areas, bananas, pawpaws and mangoes are common garden trees.

Where people live by the sea, they supplement their diet with seafood. French and Italian migrants are seen collecting sea urchins around Sydney's beaches at low tide. The whitebait season in October and November is a big event on New Zealand's South Island when hundreds of fishermen stretch nets across the river mouths. Local whitebait is different from the British variety, being the larval stage of a native New Zealand fish. It is delicious in an omelette (see recipe). When making the omelette, if you want to use more fish than the recipe suggests, just incorporate it into the egg mixture, allowing at least a quarter cup for each person.

Weekend fishing trips are part of the local lifestyle. Country people often drive long distances to the coast to fish, returning with their "esky" or cooler filled with fish for their freezers.

Three-quarters of the people in Papua New Guinea practice subsistence farming of traditional foods such as *taro,* sweet potato, sago and pigs – an estimated 20,000 tons of pork is raised annually for consumption and ceremonies. For climatic and technical reasons Papua New Guinea is still a long way from being self-sufficient. Food imports run to thousands of tons, mainly because of the demand from the large white expatriate population.

# New Zealand whitebait omelette

**You will need:**
½ cup of whitebait (or white fleshed fish)
2 eggs
2 tablespoons of water
salt and freshly-ground black pepper
1 tablespoon of butter
lemon juice
parsley and lemon to garnish

**What to do:**
(1) First prepare the fish by placing it in a saucepan of boiling water. Swirl gently with a fork until just cooked and the fish is white. Do not boil violently, or it will break up. Drain the fish and place on paper towel. (2) In a small bowl, whisk the eggs with a pinch of salt and the water. Heat the butter in a heavy pan and, when sizzling, add the egg mixture. Be sure it cooks without burning, lifting occasionally with a wooden spatula. (3) When the egg has partially set on top, spoon the fish onto half the omelette. Add lemon juice and black pepper to taste. Finally flip over the plain half of the omelette, enclosing the fish. (4) Serve immediately garnished with parsley and a lemon wedge. A tomato, lettuce and onion salad is a good accompaniment to this dish. Serves 1.

**Safety note:** Be very careful when putting the fish in the boiling water – and when taking it out. Ask an adult to help.

*Many people catch their own food. The great reef off of New Caledonia yields an abundant supply of fish and lobster.*

Primary industry centers on stock raising, agriculture and fisheries. An estimated 128,000 cattle are grazed along with some sheep. Food crops are rice, grown in the dry Morobe Province, coffee, fruits and vegetables and cocoa intercropped with coconuts. Papua New Guinea's 700,000 sq km (270,000 sq mi) of clear waters produce year-long catches of mackerel and tuna. *Bêches-de-mer*, or sea slugs, and shark fin are exported to Asian countries. Inland rivers, like the Fly and the Sepik, teem with fresh-water crayfish and shrimp while coastal bays and reefs abound in fish, crabs, and shellfish. Fishing is still mainly by traditional methods, but joint enterprises with Japan, Britain and Australia are now improving the catch.

New Caledonia runs beef cattle on northern ranches and is self-supporting in dairy products and some vegetables. No commercial farming is carried out in any of Australia's island territories. With good harbors and freezing facilities, fishing is a potential source of income. Norfolk Island practices a limited amount of horticulture but relies on most of its foodstuffs being flown from the mainland.

# Selling the food

Getting the food to market quickly is of vital importance in the hot Australasian climate.

A constant problem for food producers in Australia is the vast distances between the country properties where the food is grown and the urban areas where it is sold. Some cattle stations lie more than a thousand kilometers (600 mi) from any significant settlement. New Zealand's mountains and rivers make it difficult to build roads and railroads, while Papua New Guinea faces further problems with its rugged terrain.

Communications in Australia were not easy from the outset when explorers had to scramble over the eastern range to reach the inland plains. Rivers were shallow and unreliable for transporting goods; even large streams drained into inland salt lakes.

With its population still concentrated on the coast, Australia's problems have not changed, but it

*Huge road-trains, like the one in this picture, transport cattle to market in Australia. This one was photographed on the Stuart Highway, south of Alice Springs.*

*Sydney's Pyrmont Fish Market attracts big crowds. This woman is buying live Queensland mud crabs.*

has developed an efficient transportation system to move produce. All major towns are linked by road, rail and air services while some 66 ports handle coastal shipping. Long freight trains haul goods across the continent on the trans-Australia railroad. Road-trains, some more than 50 m (160 ft) in length, carry livestock. The 3,000 km (1,900 mi) Stuart Highway links Darwin with Adelaide, via remote towns like Alice Springs.

Lying so far from its trading partners in Europe, North America, the Middle East and Japan made it necessary to develop fast shipping services from Australasian ports. The greatest potential for further growth lies in refrigerated and frozen foodstuffs. Refrigerated container vessels from New Zealand take exports all over the world. New Zealand lamb is eaten in 100 different countries.

Large fruit and vegetable markets are a feature of most towns. Auckland's Victoria Market caters to the city's huge Polynesian population. Sydney's Paddy's Market sells a great variety of temperate and tropical goods. Noumea and Port Moresby have busy markets selling upcountry produce. Seafood is either auctioned or sold at local fish markets. Sydney's Pyrmont Fish Market offers more than a hundred varieties of fish, shellfish and crustaceans.

Most of the wholesale market traders in Australia are Chinese while retail food shops, grocers and delicatessens are owned by Italians, Greeks and Lebanese.

Supermarkets are located in most suburbs and rural towns. Specialty food shops are found in the more cosmopolitan cities of Sydney and Melbourne. Sydney's best known department store, David Jones, has introduced a food department on the lines of Harrods in London.

At the bottom end of the growing and selling scale is the small-time farmer who approaches his customers direct from a roadside stand. Such stands are often unattended (you put your money in an "honesty box") and sell items like pumpkins, honey and bottled oysters. Where berries thrive on the North Island of New Zealand, signs announce that you may "Pick Your Own."

# The nutritional value of food

The diet of white Australians, 200 years after the first landing there in 1788, still includes almost no indigenous foods of which many are an excellent source of protein, vitamins and energy.

Witchetty grubs and mangrove worms are high in protein. Kangaroo meat, low in fat and cholesterol, contains only one calorie per gram, compared to three to five calories per gram in beef. Aboriginal tribes in the central desert survived for weeks eating only woolly-butt grass seeds, which are high in protein, energy and trace elements.

Many urban Aborigines have suffered malnutrition and other deficiencies related to a poor diet by abandoning traditional "bush tucker" for western fast-foods. And while the superb, pollution-free environment in the Antipodes grows first-rate food and livestock, the average Australian and New Zealand diet is not always ideal for good health.

Many people are overweight from eating too much junk food, rich in carbohydrates and saturated fats, and from eating more than is necessary. In addition to three substantial meals a day, many people also consume large morning and afternoon teas. While a high-fiber diet is known to aid digestion, the average Australian's daily intake – mainly in breakfast cereals – is double the ideal level for good health.

Steak is always well done, vegetables well boiled. Nutrients in meat and vegetables are usually destroyed in the cooking. In the cities where women work, there is a demand for "ready-to-heat"

*The Australasians eat lots of cereal.*

*Australasians eat a lot of meat. Here a New Zealand family enjoys a barbecue.*

gourmet meals, readily available and easy to carry home. Most families stock up once a week with pre-packed goods from the local supermarket.

In Sydney and Melbourne, people are more in touch with new foods and new ways of cooking. Stir-fry cooking with a *wok* is used at home. Bistros specializing in charcoal grills which seal the nutrients in are popular. Although Australians are big meat-eaters – 38.8 kg (85.5 lb) of beef and veal and 21.9 kg (48 lb) of lamb a head per year – fresh fish is gaining favor. Seafood, which is high in protein, with very little fat, is an excellent source of niacin, needed for energy and a healthy skin. Oysters have twice as much iron as red meat and

are eaten by the dozen.

One strange aspect about Australia is that while fast-food chains enjoy record sales, there are probably more health-food stores than in Britain which has five times the Australian population. Fresh fruit salad and yogurt take-outs are popular, but it will take time and education to displace meat pies, hot dogs and ice creams. Australians lick their way through 200 million gallons of ice cream a year! Sugar consumption of 45 kg (100 lb) per person is the highest in the world.

New Zealand produces a wide range of health foods from dried goats' milk and soybean milk to organically grown vegetables. Local mills produce a variety of flours such as stoneground wheat and rye flour, along with specialty flours made from rice, soybeans and barley. As in Australia, health food shops sell snacks such as dried fruits and muesli bars, but New Zealanders also nibble on junk food snacks.

Honey and honey-related products are well-known exports from New Zealand along with cereals, food yeasts, wheatgerm and bran. Local fruits are the basis of a variety of beverages with no additives or artificial preservatives. Both countries have established reputations for dietary supplements and all forms of vitamins and minerals.

# Mango mayonnaise with ginger

**You will need:**

1 carton of sour cream

3 large slices of canned mango, or 1 fresh mango, finely-chopped

½ inch piece of fresh ginger root, finely-grated

1 teaspoon of finely-grated lemon rind

1½ tablespoons of fresh lemon-juice

**What to do:**

Combine all the ingredients, mix well and allow to chill before use. Serve with any cold seafood (it goes especially well with smoked trout).

*Superb cuts of salmon from commercial farms in Tasmania. Only the best and freshest foods are sold.*

# Cooking equipment and methods

The indigenous peoples of Australasia were clever in turning various items into useful cooking and eating utensils.

The Aborigines of tropical Australia used conch shells for carrying water by means of attached rope handles. The huge bailer shells, found on exposed reefs, were for boiling water and cooking things like *pippi*-soup. Smaller, discarded shells were used to line underground ovens. Other shells were sharpened to be used as cutting edges.

Different techniques were used for cooking the various foods. The most common were roasting on the coals, cooking in the embers, steaming in a pit and boiling. The roasting technique was used to cook the flesh of kangaroos, goannas, turtles and large fish. The carcass was flung on the fire to singe its fur. When the carcass swelled, the fur was scraped off. The meat was then roasted slowly, although people were often so hungry that they ate theirs rare.

Cooking in an earth or sand pit lined with stones, shells or coral and covered with paper bark or banana leaves to retain the steam was another common method of cooking vegetables, large fish and pigs in Australasia. Foods such as yams, or plantain bananas, were wrapped in parcels of leaves and steamed directly on the stones. The food was served on large, flat leaves from the banana or spear tree, or on plates woven from bark. In central Australia, flat stones were used to grind grass seeds into flour for making damper (bush bread). These methods are still used by Aborigines living in the bush.

Simple cooking utensils used by the Maoris were pounders and stone mortars, oven stones, woven fiber mats for covering the oven, shells for scraping, gourds for holding water and woven baskets for gathering sweet potatoes.

While there were countless ways of preparing food, the Maoris, like the Aborigines, used only two or three ways of cooking it. The most common was steaming in an

*A bushwalker lighting a fire to boil the billy while his parrot watches.*

*No cooking utensils are needed for this* bougna, *or underground meal, in Melanesian New Caledonia – only a shovel to dig the hole. Raked out, and cool, the food (pork, yams and sweet potatoes) is eaten in the fingers.*

underground oven called a *hangi*. This remains a popular way to cook for a large number of relatives and friends in New Zealand. Great efforts go into the preparation and lining of a *hangi*, with different layers of vegetation used for different types of foods. Steaming generally takes anything from two to six hours, the items being removed and unwrapped with great celebration and rejoicing. Grilling, or *rorerore*, is used to prepare quick, small meals such as skewered fish, or birds cooked over the low coals. Shellfish are also cooked this way in their own juices. *Kohua*, or boiling, in the early days was rare because, while skilled at sculpture, the Maoris did not make pottery. Heating was achieved by dropping a red hot stone into a wooden bowl containing water and the item to be cooked. Chopped yam and sweet potato, cooked in unsalted water, cooled and then mashed, were added to the first stage of leaven in making Maori bread.

The cooking equipment used by swagmen and drovers in the Australian bush is kept minimal for easy mobility. Swagmen are occasionally seen walking along an outback track with an enamel cup for tea, a blackened billy-can and a damper tray dangling from their backs. A drover, or stockman, ties

# Tomato pie

**You will need:**

8 medium well-ripened tomatoes, skinned
1 large onion, thinly-sliced
butter
salt and freshly-ground black pepper
2 cups breadcrumbs, made from roughly broken stale brown bread

**What to do:**

Pre-heat the oven to 350°F and grease a small pie dish with the butter. (1) Place a layer of thinly-sliced tomatoes on the bottom, cover with the onion and repeat. Add salt and pepper and fill the dish, finishing with a layer of tomato. (2) Top with the breadcrumbs, add several good blobs of butter and cook until the top is golden brown, about 40 minutes. Be careful the top does not burn. (3) Serve as an accompaniment to roast lamb and vegetables, or with barbecued meat, potatoes and a green salad. Serves 4.

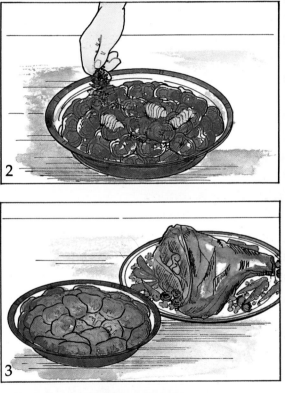

them to his saddle.

Essential items in the old days were a billy, a piece of fencing wire which doubled as a toasting fork or a prong for grilling meat, a rolling pin for making dough and a damper tray. A bush knife served to cut an animal's throat as well as to hack off hunks of damper. The green eucalyptus twig, essential to making tea, was plucked from a nearby gum tree.

Except for a charcoal barbecue you need nothing special to cook typical Australasian-style recipes. Your own kitchen equipment will do, but a blender, *wok*, tongs and a thick-bottomed pan will be useful.

# Traditional foods and customs

Australia's most famous product, the brown yeast extract known as "Vegemite," was introduced by the American Kraft company after the war. Why it became such a success here and nowhere else is not known, but, raised on Vegemite sandwiches, even adult Australians feel deprived without it. Harrods keeps a stock especially for London's Australian expatriates.

While early recipe books, such as the *Country Women's Association Cook Book*, list common British recipes that were popular, other dishes are genuinely part of the Australian heritage.

Shearer's stew with jumbuck dumplings is a uniquely Australian meal (see recipe on p.30), along with parakeet pie (an early pioneers' mixture of small parrots, strips of

*Chocolate-coated sponge cake squares or lamingtons. Other* dinki-di *dishes are damper, and pavlova.*

beef, hard-boiled eggs and stock baked in a pastry pie). Other *dinki-di* dishes are carpetbag steak (a fillet of beef containing a pocket of rock oysters), kangaroo-tail soup (once served on the national airline), parsnip patties, fried scones or "Johnny cakes" and bush-bread, or damper. Two of Australia's own desserts are named after famous women performers: the meringue topped with cream and passion fruit after Pavlova, the Russian ballerina (see recipe on p.31), and peach Melba, created by L'Escoffier at London's Savoy Hotel in 1892 in honor of the Melbourne opera singer, Dame Nellie Melba. The small, chocolate-iced sponge cakes known as lamingtons are said to have been invented by Bert Sash, chef at the Esplanade Hotel in Fremantle, Western Australia (see page 41).

People traditionally consume large breakfasts in Australia. It is not uncommon for a farmer rounding up cattle or sheep to start the day with a huge plate of steak and eggs. Fish appears on some breakfast menus in tropical Queensland.

Snacks have a permanent place in local eating habits. Australia's most famous in-between meal is a meat pie filled with chopped meat and gravy and topped with lots of

# Shearer's stew with jumbuck dumplings

**You will need:**

1 tablespoon of oil
1 tablespoon of butter
2 to 2¼ lb of lamb, chopped and dusted in flour
3 onions, quartered
3 parsnips, sliced
3 carrots, thickly-sliced
2 sticks of celery, chopped
meat or vegetable stock
3 tablespoons of parsley, chopped
1 teaspoon of mixed herbs
1 tablespoon of Worcestershire sauce
salt and freshly-ground black pepper

for the dumplings:
2 cups of self-rising flour
1 tablespoon of parsley, chopped
salt and plenty of freshly-ground black pepper
about ¾ cup of milk, or water

**What to do:**

(1) Heat the oil and butter in a large, heavy pan and brown the lamb on all sides. Push to one side and sauté the onions until transparent. Transfer to a heavy iron pot or a casserole dish. (2) Add all the other ingredients and cover with the stock. Simmer on a low heat until the lamb is tender, about 2–2½ hours. (3) Add the flour, parsley, salt and pepper to a large mixing-bowl and stir in the milk, or water, until the dough forms a soft dropping consistency. (4) Dust your hands with flour, gently roll into small dough-balls and place on top of the stew while it is still simmering. Cover and cook for about 15 minutes before you are ready to serve the meal. Serves 6–8.

# Pavlova

**You will need:**
4 egg whites
1 cup of fine white sugar
2 teaspoons of vinegar
1 tablespoon of cornstarch
1 teaspoon of vanilla essence
1 carton of whipping cream
passion fruit, strawberries or bananas,
   sliced
a little cornstarch and confectioners'
   sugar for dusting

**What to do:**
Grease a cookie sheet and dust with confectioners' sugar and cornstarch. (1) Beat the egg whites until very stiff, then slowly add the sugar, beating until the mixture is even stiffer. (2) Fold in the cornstarch, vinegar and vanilla and pile high on the cookie sheet to 7 to 8 inches across. Bake in a slow oven 1–1½ hours until firm. Do not allow to color on top. (3) When it is cool, spread with the whipped cream and passion fruit and either strawberries, or bananas. Serves about 6–8.

**Safety note:** Ask an adult to take the pavlova out of the oven for you.

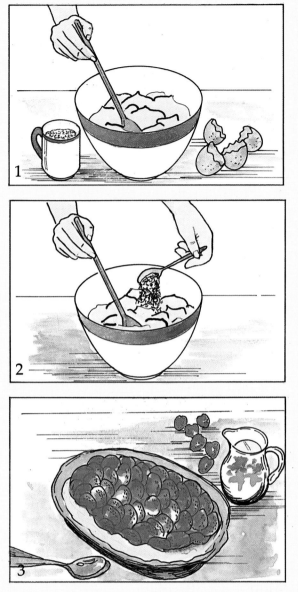

"Pick-Me-Up" tomato sauce. The peculiarly named "pluto pups" (frankfurters speared with a cane stick and fried in crispy batter) are also a tradition.

Also peculiar to the Antipodes are the following favorites: jaffas (chocolate-coated orange-sherbet balls), milkshakes (milk caramels), minties (mint caramels), fan-tales (chocolate-coated caramels, which are wrapped in wax-paper biographies of movie stars) and violet crumble-bars (delicious chocolate-coated honeycomb).

Innovative restaurants in Sydney and Melbourne are devising exciting new dishes based on *nouvelle cuisine* and Asian cooking methods but using local products. Whether such things as warm salads, *barramundi bulla-bulla* and wattle pavlova will find a permanent place in modern Australian cookery remains to be seen.

Eager to cast off a heritage of dull, rather heavy English dishes, chefs in New Zealand are also utilizing the excellent local ingredients to create new recipes. Until now, typical dishes were bluff oysters, whitebait omelettes and fritters, roast venison and the rather oily Southland mutton-bird made into fishy-flavored mutton-bird pies. Restaurants are now experimenting with new recipes such as fish served with butter and tamarillo sauce and rack of lamb cooked in a berry *coulis* instead of brown gravy. A typical appetizer might be green-lip mussels with herb and tomato dressing.

As the Caldoche in New Caledonia is politically one of the departments of France, local cooking is French – whether Parisian or Lyonnaise varies according to the chef.

For Australasia's indigenous inhabitants, food cooked in underground pits or in the embers of a fire is as old as human settlement in the region. An offshoot of outdoor cooking is the Australasian barbecue enjoyed on a Saturday evening or a Sunday lunchtime by at least half the population from Noumea to Perth.

The rather odd aspect about eating habits is that few opportunities exist for dining outdoors at restaurants. Sydney, situated on one of the world's most beautiful harbors, has less than a dozen restaurants where diners can enjoy the view. Only Doyle's, established as a small hut in the 1800s, serves seafood by the water. A daily weather forecast appears on the menu.

Introduced by the Italians and Viennese, "coffee-lounges" (cafés) are traditional places to enjoy

*"Runny meat pie" with tomato sauce is a traditional Australian snack.*

# Green-lip mussels with herb and tomato dressing

**You will need:**

50 green-lip mussels (substitute ordinary mussels, as large as possible)

¼ cup of dry white wine

2–3 bay leaves

For the dressing:

2 tablespoons of olive oil

4 green onions (scallions), finely-chopped

2 medium tomatoes, skinned and finely-diced

1 teaspoon each of parsley and marjoram, finely-chopped

a little salt and freshly-ground pepper to taste

**What to do:**

Clean the mussels well under cold running water. Put half the mussels in a large saucepan with the bay leaves, add the wine, cover and bring to the boil. (1) As the mussels open, lift out with tongs and place in a bowl. Now cook the remaining mussels. (2) Strain the liquid through cheesecloth and set aside. When the mussels are quite cold, remove the top shell together with any sand. Arrange on a slightly concave plate and set aside. (3) Heat the oil in a small pan and briefly sauté the green onions. Remove and allow to cool. Add the tomatoes and marjoram. Stir in sufficient strained mussel stock to bring the dressing to a pouring consistency. (4) Add the parsley and spoon over the mussels. To allow the flavor to permeate the mussels, cover with plastic wrap and allow to stand at room temperature for 2 hours. Serves 4.

*Whenever possible, Australians and New Zealanders eat outdoors. Pictured is a pub at Watson's Bay on Sydney Harbor where lobster is on the menu.*

brunch or a snack. Sydney has more cafés than Naples or Vienna. They are usually prettily-decorated places serving cakes, coffee, sandwiches and other snacks popular with office-workers.

Picnic race-meetings are an annual country custom in Australian towns. Days before the program in which their husbands are likely to be riding wild bush horses, country wives are busy cooking. Lunch of cold sausages, chicken, paté, quiches, salads and damper is eaten from a hamper in the back of the family's station wagon.

# Drinks

People have quenched their thirst with tea since the earliest days of settlement in the Antipodes. "Boiling the billy" is part of Australia's Outback heritage. Tea leaves are thrown into the billy of boiling water and, after being allowed to stew for several minutes, are stirred with a green eucalyptus twig, said to give a true "bush flavor." Since fresh milk was not readily available in the old days,

*Every country town in Australia has a "milk bar."*

tea was either drunk black or with condensed milk.

Today, coffee has almost replaced tea as the traditional beverage in the cities, but in the country people still drink tea morning, noon and night. The French in New Caledonia have always been coffee drinkers. People in Papua New Guinea drink their own high-grown, *arabica* coffee.

In Australia and New Zealand, where dairying is an important industry, people drink a great deal of fresh milk. The average intake

per person in Australia is estimated at 102.5 liters (27 gals) a year.

In addition to "milk bars" selling milkshakes, snacks and desserts, there are bars selling fresh fruit juices made from citrus fruits and tropical juices such as mango, pineapple, guava, kiwi fruit and tamarillo (a delicious, slightly tart species of New Zealand tree tomato). About 30 percent of New Zealand's crop of pears and apples is processed into juice. The Australian island state of Tasmania is famous for cider.

Soft drinks made from fruit juices, for example, "Passiona" and "Mango and Orange," are also popular; so are brands like 7-Up and Diet Cola. The sale of soft drinks in Australia exceeds $1.8 billion per year.

Antipodeans are beer drinkers from 'way back. During the gold rush, Kalgoorlie in Western Australia had 93 pubs (bars) and 8 breweries for a population of 30,000. Some rural towns in Australia may only have a pub. "Foster's," "Swan" and "Castlemaine XXXX" beer are exported to countries all over the world.

In recent times, Antipodean wine has also become popular abroad. In 1840, the French navigator Durmont d'Urville remarked on the excellence of New Zealand wine. In 1986, a small vineyard in New Zealand named Hunter's Wines won the gold medal at the London Sunday *Times* Wine Show.

New Zealand's vineyards are spread across the North Island. Hawke Bay is one of the best producers, but in their search for cooler climates, local wine makers have also gone to Marlborough in the South Island where summers are dry but not too hot. *Sauvignon Blanc* is the grape that has made the biggest impression among a number of fruity white wines. As in Australia, European migrants, in particular the Italians, French, Yugoslavs and Germans, have lent their expertise to the New Zealand wine industry.

The Australian wine industry dates from the 1800s when a settler named James Busby planted the first vines in the Hunter River Valley, north of Sydney. Today most states are involved in wine making. The best known regions are Pokolbin in the Hunter, the Barossa Valley in South Australia, the Yarra Valley in Victoria and the

*Afternoon tea is an old ritual, especially among country people.*

The harvest of Shiraz grapes on the Wyndham Estate, in Pokolbin in the Hunter River area of New South Wales. New Zealand wines have become internationally known.

Swan Valley and Margaret River region in Western Australia.

Australian *Chardonnay*, *Cabernet* and *Riesling* have a well-deserved international reputation. Being in the Southern Hemisphere is an advantage to marketing, with the vintage being six months ahead of that in Europe.

BYOs ("bring your own" restaurants which have no liquor license) are common in both Australia and New Zealand. People bring their own wine, some diners sending theirs in advance to be chilled, if necessary. Australia produces several types of champagne, among which Great Western Brut is popular.

# The immigrants' influence on food

The immigration of thousands of Europeans, Asians and Pacific Islanders to Australia and New Zealand has had a profound effect on local eating habits. "Aussies" and "Kiwis" are also traveling more and returning with a new taste for more exotic foreign foods.

The Italians were among the first arrivals during the postwar years in Australia. They introduced pasta dishes, *risotto* and *cappucino* coffee and later a more sophisticated style of northern Italian cuisine which has become popular in trend-setting restaurants.

Australia's big Turkish community settled mainly in Melbourne and opened ethnic restaurants and *doner kebab* take-outs. A flood of Greek immigrants brightened up menus with dishes like *moussaka* and desserts such as the honey-nut pastry called *baklava*. They also improved dull local salads by adding *feta* cheese, black olives and olive oil.

Most milk bars and many food

*The French influence in New Caledonia is strong. Here boys on the Isle of Pines bring home fresh* baguettes.

*Many Asians who have come to live in Australia have set up restaurant businesses in both big cities and country towns.*

American-style fast-foods have also been a powerful influence since the first "Kentucky Fried Chicken" reached Australia in 1968. An estimated 35 million "finger-lickin" chicken meals were sold last year, while the Pizza Hut chain sold over 8 million pizzas. Surveys show Australians buy two to three family-sized take-outs each week. Barnacle Bill is a popular seafood take-out chain in South Australia selling packaged pavlova along with battered and fried whiting.

The influence of the immigrant population can also be seen in stores. Butchers who once sold only sausages and lamb now offer offal and *shish kebabs*; bakeries offer *khoubz*, packs of flat Arab bread, and, although unpopular fifteen years ago, octopus and "yabbies" are popular at the fish markets.

It was inevitable that Australian taste should change with now over a million immigrants from over 100 different countries. What has happened to the different immigrant groups, however, is equally interesting. They have adopted the local penchant for barbecues: Sydney's National Park is taken over by Lebanese cooking kebabs on a Sunday; Yugoslavs picnic by the beach at Cronulla, and you are quite likely to find Maoris or Cook Islanders preparing a *hangi* by Botany Bay. The different groups' ethnic cuisines have been enhanced by Australasia's high-quality local ingredients.

stores are run by immigrants, but while a Greek café or a Chinese restaurant may still be the only place to dine out in a country town, Australia's cities are packed with cosmopolitan restaurants. Perth, whose population is a little more than a million people has over 1,500 restaurants.

The most recent immigrants, Lebanese and Vietnamese refugees, have also entered the food and catering trades. The Sydney suburb of Cabramatta, known as "Little Vietnam," serves better food than you can find in Saigon. Lebanese restaurants are a feature of the inner city.

# Festive foods

Christmas is the most important festive occasion celebrated by Australasia's largely Christian communities. Although it falls in summer, nostalgia for a wintry homeland, which many have never visited, sees Australians building log fires, decorating trees and spraying their windows with pressure-pack snow. Santa's reindeer are sometimes seen as kangaroos pulling a sleigh of gifts!

Most families sit down to a traditional Anglo-Saxon dinner when the temperature may be 35°C (95°F). To start there is smoked coral trout, or Atlantic salmon, followed by roast turkey with bread sauce and baked vegetables including pumpkin. Dessert may be either plum pudding with brandy butter or tropical fruit salad.

Christmas falls during the long school vacation when families camping in a tent, or a camper, eat a similar traditional meal under beach umberellas. During the week

*These men are cooking sausages by the Yarra River in Melbourne, Victoria. Most festivals and public holidays are celebrated with a barbecue.*

# Lamingtons

**You will need:**
one stick plus 2½ tablespoons of butter
¾ cup of sugar
2 cups plus 3 tablespoons of self-rising
    flour
2 eggs
4 tablespoons of milk
a few drops of vanilla essence

for the icing:
3½ oz of butter
1 tablespoon of cocoa
1¾ cups of confectioners' sugar
about 7 oz of shredded or flaked coconut
a few drops of vanilla essence

**What to do:**
(1) Cream the butter and sugar, add the beaten eggs with the milk and vanilla and finally the sifted flour. Pour into a flat, greased pan and bake for 30 minutes in a moderately hot oven. (2) Turn out onto a cake rack, allow to cool, then slice into medium-sized squares. Ice the following day. To make the icing, cream the butter and confectioners' sugar and add the cocoa, mixing with a little water and the vanilla. (3) Dip the squares of sponge cake in the icing and coat well before rolling in the coconut. (4) Serve with tea at afternoon-tea time.

*Bringing up the* hangi. *New Zealanders prepare this traditional Maori feast on holidays and family gatherings when a large number of people gather together.*

preceding December 25, children may be seen singing carols outside the big city stores.

Children's birthdays are highlighted by a multi-colored marble cake or a rich pavlova. Other party delicacies are lamingtons, butterfly cakes and bread and butter covered with colored sprinkles.

Public holidays are celebrated with a barbecue, either portable or one built in the yard. Grilled steak, chops and sausages are commonly eaten on such an occasion, when Maoris may prepare a

*hangi* for as many as a hundred people. Ethnic communities in Australia celebrate their own national days with feasting and traditional dancing.

The Caldoche in New Caledonia celebrate Bastille Day with lunch in an outdoor restaurant or a picnic on their boat. The menu features dishes like quiche, paté, salads and *poisson cru*, a local Melanesian way of preparing raw fish with fresh lime-juice and coconut milk. Fish and lobsters speared by the men are cooked on the coral reef. *Bougnas* or native feasts in New Caledonia and similar feasts in New Guinea, when hundreds of pigs are slaughtered, usually mark local occasions and sports events.

# Poisson Cru

**You will need:**

2 lb of game fish – tuna, bonito or other fish with flesh that is red and firm, as distinct from a white fish like flounder

6 limes

1 onion, skinned and sliced

2 cups of pure coconut milk

**What to do:**

(1) Skin, bone and cut the fish into chunks. Marinate in fresh lime-juice for 30 minutes to 2 hours (until the flesh is blanched). (2) Transfer to a dish, sprinkle with the onion and pour the coconut-milk over it, turning well. (3) Serve.

To obtain the coconut-milk (canned or pressed coconut will not do), grate the white flesh of one coconut. Place this in a piece of cheesecloth and place the cheesecloth in a large bowl with the corners hanging out. Pour 1 quart of boiling water on the coconut, allow to cool a little. Then taking the ends, wring out well to obtain a milky liquid.

**Safety note:** You will need a sharp knife to skin, bone and cut the fish, so ask an adult to do it for you.

Like the Kanaks, Australian Aborigines have no cause to celebrate alien European events. However in the old days, various seasonal changes, the end of the monsoon season, or the goose-egg laying time in Arnhem Land, for example, were marked by feasting and *corroborees* (ceremonial tattooing and dancing).

Among the most extraordinary occasions were the great moth feasts in the Bogong Mountains, near Canberra. During the height of the summer, hundreds of people from different tribes would meet to eat the large-winged moths that collected in caves. Bogong moths, which are described as having a "walnut flavor," are apparently very nutritious and are marketed, along with other native foods like witchetty grubs and lillypilly fruit, by the "Bush Tucker Supply Company" in Sydney.

Aborigines, who are excellent stockmen, are usually among the contestants in rodeos held in country towns like Wingham and Raymond Terrace on the central coast of New South Wales. In addition to roughriding events, most rural shows feature country produce.

*A huge agricultural exhibit at Sydney's Royal Easter Show, the biggest in the South Pacific, celebrates the bi-centenary of the first settlement.*

Sydney's Royal Easter Show, held during ten days at Easter, is one of the biggest food and livestock shows in the world. The vast "Food and Agricultural Pavilion" is noted for spectacular exhibits of the finest produce from every state in Australia. Prime livestock from all over the bush competes for "Grand Champion Awards" when stud fees run into hundreds of thousands of Australian dollars. A feature of the show is take-out food bars selling everything from billy-tea and damper to "pluto pups."

New Zealand is also noted for rural shows where people from both countries participate in shrimp and oyster-eating competitions. The town of Dargaville in the North Island of New Zealand holds a sweet-potato festival.

# Glossary

**Aborigine** (Australian) Original native inhabitant of Australia.

**Antipodes** Lands at extremes of the world. In this context, Australia and New Zealand.

**Billabong** A river branch, forming a stagnant pool or backwater.

**Billy** (or billy-can) A cylindrical metal container used for cooking, making tea, etc.

**Bulldust** "Strine" (Australian slang) for the deep, red dust of the interior.

**Bush** Shrubby or wooded, untilled district.

**Bush Tucker** "Strine" for Aborigines' food, or bush food.

**Caldoche** A white New Caledonian descended from original settlers.

**Coolamon** A wooden bowl used by Aborigines for carrying food.

**Damper** Unleavened "bush bread" baked in wood ashes.

**Damper tray** A flat tin for preparing damper.

**Deadheart** "Strine" referring to the great empty center of Australia.

**Dinki-di** "Strine" for the real thing, the original.

**Dreamtime** The "golden age" at the beginning of time in the mythology of some Aborigines.

**Drover** A cattle dealer. A person who drives cattle to market.

**Eski** In Australia, a polystyrene cooler for keeping food and drinks cold.

**Hangi** A Maori oven.

**Jumbuck** Aborigine's word for sheep.

**Kanaks** South Sea Islanders, especially those once employed as forced labor in Australia.

**Mallee** Scrub country, mainly wattle or acacia in Australia.

**Maori** A member of an aboriginal Polynesian race in New Zealand.

**Pippi** A bivalve mollusc, valued for soup by Australian Aborigines.

**Road-train** A huge truck with several trailers; it can be over 50 m (164 ft) long.

**Scurvy** A disease caused by lack of vitamin C in the diet.

**Southerly buster** A sudden wind, often with rain, in southeastern Australia. It may lower the temperature many degrees in a matter of minutes.

**Strine** Australian slang or colloquial speech.

**Swagman** A tramp.

**Taboo** Forbidden within a society.

**Tucker** "Strine" for food.

**Whitebait** Small silvery-white fish.

**Witchetty grub** A large white beetle or moth larvae, eaten by Australian Aborigines.

**Yabbies** Aborigine's word for small freshwater crayfish.

| Typical Australian or New Zealand family menu | | | |
|---|---|---|---|
| **Breakfast:** | cereal, probably *Weet-Bix*<br>eggs<br>toast with jam, honey or *Vegemite* | **Afternoon tea:** | cakes (homemade in the country), tea |
| **Morning tea:** | coffee or tea with biscuits and cheese | **Dinner:** | soup<br>grilled chops and vegetables or fish and "chips" (french fries)<br>ice cream and canned fruit or a pudding |
| **Lunch:** | sandwiches, pizza, meat pie | | |

# Further Reading

Armitage, Ronda, *New Zealand* (Bookwright Press, 1988)

Arnold, Caroline, *Australia Today* (Franklin Watts, 1987)

Ball, John, *We Live in New Zealand* (Bookwright Press, 1984)

Burns, Geoff, *Take a Trip to New Zealand* (Franklin Watts, 1983)

Ellis, Rennie, *We Live In Australia* (Bookwright Press, 1983)

Gunner, Emily and Shirley McConky, *A Family in Australia* (Bookwright Press, 1985)

Lye, Keith, *Asia and Australasia* (Gloucester Press, 1987)

Pepper, Susan, *Passport to Australia* (Franklin Watts, 1987)

# Index

## Acknowledgments

Christine Osborne would like to thank the following for help with research: Inter-Continental Sydney, Tourism Australia and Philippine Airlines. Her mother Joy Osborne of Taree and sister Julia Osborne of Wingham were an invaluable source of information on early colonial food in Australia.

All photographs were supplied by Christine Osborne except the following: Chris Fairclough 4, 10, 12, 13, 24, 39; Mary Evans Picture Library 9. The map on page 5 is by Malcolm Walker. All step-by-step recipe illustrations are by Juliette Nicholson.